Brussels, the Gentle Monster

THE GERMAN LIST

HANS MAGNUS
ENZENSBERGER

Brussels, the Gentle Monster
or the Disenfranchisement of Europe

TRANSLATED BY MARTIN CHALMERS

LONDON NEW YORK CALCUTTA

 **GOETHE-INSTITUT**

This publication was supported by
a grant from the Goethe-Institut India

Seagull Books, 2011

Hans Magnus Enzensberger,
Sanftes Monster Brüssel oder Die Entmündigung Europas
© Suhrkamp Verlag, Berlin, 2011

First published in English by Seagull Books, 2011.

English translation © Martin Chalmers, 2011

ISBN-13   978 0 85742 023 7

British Library Cataloguing-in-Publication Data
A catalogue record for this book is available
from the British Library

Typeset by Seagull Books, Calcutta, India
Printed and bound by Hyam Enterprises, Calcutta, India

CONTENTS

This essay was completed in January 2011.
I would like to thank the Sonning Foundation in Copenhagen
and the Prix de Littérature Européenne in Cognac, who not
only gave me money but also encouraged me to write this book.

H. M. E.

I

Praise Where it's Due

Good news is rare; which is why it's a good idea to begin with it, even if a real reporter prefers the bad.

The most important first: there have been only a very few decades in the history of our continent in which peace has reigned. Since 1945, there has not been a single armed conflict between states belonging to the European Union. Almost a whole lifetime without war! That's an anomaly of which this continent can be proud.

We can also be glad about a whole number of other comforts which are not a matter of life and death. They are by now taken so much for granted that we hardly notice them any more. People younger than 60 will have no idea how difficult it was, after the Second World War, to set foot in a neighbouring country. A journey abroad was impossible without a prolonged struggle with bureaucracy. Anyone who wanted to cross a border had to produce authenticated letters of invitation, fill out visa applications in triplicate in order to request residence permits, overcome complicated foreign-exchange control regulations and a dozen other hurdles. If one wanted to order a book from abroad, that meant an elaborate procedure involving the main customs office. If one was expecting a money transfer from France or wanted to pay a bill from Spain, then that was equivalent to an act of sovereignty which could not be completed without a collection of official stamps. Today, all of that is no more than a fading memory. Anyone holding a passport of most member countries of the European Union can live wherever he or she wants in the Union without queuing up at an Aliens Registration Office in order to get hold of a residence or work permit. It is even possible, with a few exceptions, to plug in an electrical appliance without packing a whole arsenal of adapters in one's suitcase. The costs of many financial transactions have also fallen considerably in Europe, much to the chagrin of the *bureaux de change*.

In short, the process of European unification has changed everyday life for the better. Economically it was for a long time so successful that every possible and impossible membership candidate is still knocking at its gates asking to be let in.

We also have to thank our Brussels protectors for again and again valiantly taking action against cartels, oligopolies, protectionist dodges and banned subsidies.

The telephone charges! The small print in contracts intended to deceive unsuspecting consumers! The protection of non-smokers! The rip-off at cash dispensers! The Union keeps watch to ensure that, here, everything is above board.

An arduous labour that cannot be taken for granted. Because the national governments have repeatedly been only too willing to allow themselves to be bamboozled by the multinational giants of the pharmaceutical, energy, finance, foodstuffs and communications industries. These are opponents who have enormous cash resources at their disposal. They fight, no holds barred, to retain their monopoly profits, wield the threat of job losses and have become unchallenged experts in the arts of tax avoidance. Today no one country is any longer in a position to stand up to them, to resist their blackmail or even to punish them occasionally.

The European Union has also been rightly praised when it comes to other problems which can only be solved collectively. For years it has been attempting, even if without conclusive success, to put an end to the absurd patchwork which has turned control of European air space into a dangerous game of patience. The 36 different agencies which supervise it, each one with different procedures and technologies, continue to be defended with petulant tenacity by the military and civil authorities of the member states. This form of air-traffic control not only costs more than three billion euros a year but also swallows up vast amounts of fuel and leads to endless queues and delays.

The never-ending dispute over fish catch quotas also has disastrous consequences, as does the constantly postponed decision on the permanent storage of radioactive waste—problems which none of the member states alone evidently can or wants to solve. But the Union has further, quite different advantages to offer. In the remotest corners of Europe one will come across signs announcing that here something is being supported by the EU: the construction of a motorway, a bridge, a building or a research institute. Agriculture enjoys massive subsidies. Large agro-companies in particular, are generously rewarded from the biggest pot in the Brussels budget: around 59 billion euros are available for agricultural policy. Second, with 49 billion euros, comes regional policy with a total of 455 programmes. (The audit office has added a drop of bitterness to these sweeteners: according to it, when last surveyed, 36 per cent of these projects had been erroneously supported.)

Nevertheless, these are, on the whole, good deeds of which the Union can be proud. Should we then congratulate the Brussels guardians on the fine results they have achieved in so many areas despite jealously protected 'national interests'? It's not really necessary, since the European authorities are very willing to save us the trouble.

II

Official Language

No government can do without propaganda, even if the word is an unpopular one; today, a phrase like 'improved communication' is preferred. The European Union doesn't lag behind in this respect. Years ago, it was already investing heavily in promotional films and Internet portals. It subsidizes the television channel Euronews to the sum of five million euros annually, and the largely unknown radio station Euranet gets six million. The European parliament, too, has a TV channel of its own called Europarltv, for which it doesn't mind paying 10 million euros, although it has very few viewers. Much that can be seen or heard on it is reminiscent of the court circular. Self-criticism is not the strong point of our guardians.

The Commission habitually hides the national contributions to the EU budget in its Budget Report, 'because anti-Europeans could make improper use of the figures'. Anyone who wants to know too much about it counts as an enemy. The Fédération de la Fonction Publique Européenne, which represents the interests of European civil servants at the Commission, and which, in line with Brussels custom, embellishes itself with the acronym FFPE, considers that the secretiveness does not yet go far enough. Recently, it demanded in an open letter that the Commission set up a 'special unit provided with all necessary resources . . . to respond to all the disgraceful attacks which make EU staff a whipping boy'. Responsible for such slanderous attacks are 'media directed by anti-European lobbies'.

This whole PR fuss is thanks not only to the injured vanity of the civil servants but also serves to compensate for an endemic shortcoming of the integration project. It is a painful but indisputable fact that a European public sphere of debate worthy of the name does not exist. As far as the media is concerned, in each country home is where the heart is. For that reason, too, the information that reaches us from Brussels is to be treated with caution: the thinner the legitimation, the thicker the layer of PR goo.

In this uncomfortable situation there is an increasing temptation for the Union to take opinion-shaping in hand for itself. Elections, to say nothing of referendums, are irksome to all those in power; but opinion polls come in useful, at least as long as the results turn out to the client's satisfaction.

'The solution is more Europe', is the word from the Office of the Vice-President with a particular interest in communication. She refers to the results of a survey called Eurobarometer which is carried out twice a year on behalf of her office. The findings are very favourable to the Commission. 'Ninety-two per cent agreed with the statement that labour markets must be modernized and that the support of the poor and the socially excluded be given priority. Ninety per cent want an economy which uses fewer raw materials and produces fewer greenhouse gases.' A fantastic result which could no doubt even be increased had people been asked whether they were in favour of war or peace, of sickness or good health and would like to support lower earnings or vigorous wage settlements.

Matters look less triumphant if the results of other surveys are to be believed. According to them only 49 per cent of Europeans see membership of their country in a positive light and only 42 per cent trust EU institutions.

That is due, not least, to the use of language which dominates in them. Even the Treaty of Lisbon, a substitute constitution which serves as the legal basis of the Union, is distinguished by the fact that merely reading it presents even the most willing European citizen with insuperable difficulties. It is not unlike an impassable wire entanglement. Passages such as the following (from Article 2 of the Treaty) can only act as deterrents:

Throughout the Treaty: the words 'Community' and 'European Community' shall be replaced by 'Union' and any necessary grammatical changes shall be made, the words 'European Communities' shall be replaced by 'European Union', except in paragraph 6(c) of Article 299, renumbered paragraph 5(c) of Article 311a. In respect of Article 136, this amendment shall apply only to the mention of 'The Community' at the beginning of the first paragraph.

It cannot be chance that even constitutional lawyers have difficulty understanding this prose. Unfortunately, we can assume that this was indeed the intention of the authors. When, in 2008, Ireland was due to vote on the Treaty, Charles McCreevy, who was the Irish representative on the Commission, said that of the 4.2 million inhabitants of his country, less than 250 had read the work and less than 25 of those had understood it. We know what the result of the referendum was.

A comparison with the text of the American Constitution shows that it is not language alone that is being abused. The sheer size of the document speaks for itself and was only outdone by the failed Constitutional Treaty of 2004, a fat volume of 419 pages. 'Our Europe on the other hand,' wrote the poet Gottfried Benn. 'Much nonsense, cant: "The Truth", a Life's Work, 500 pages— the truth can never be as long as that!'

Other manifestations of the official language are surprising because of their deafness to history. The executive of the Union, which additionally has the sole right to initiate legislation and as 'guardian of the treaties' keeps a watch on the observance of European law by the member states, is not made up of ministers but of commissioners—as they are called in English—commissars as they are called in other European languages. We may doubt whether the inventors of the term paid any attention to what associations the word commissar arouses in Europe. Apart from the fact that in some countries what first comes to mind is a police detective, it is more generally, politically, a very loaded official title. The Soviet Union had People's Commissars from 1917 to 1946; in the Red Army, political commissars ensured that the Party line was adhered to; in Germany, between 1871 and 1945, great powers were placed in the hands of Reich Commissars; and after the German attack on the Soviet Union, Reich Commissars were in charge of the Ukraine and the so-called Ostland. The fact that the founders of the Union did not think of these obvious and quite ominous memories does not, of course, speak against their well-meant intentions; it only shows up their historical forgetfulness.

Statements by the authority also strike a curious tone, marked by an authoritarian style, as in the following text: 'In particular, enforcement activities in the period immediately following the law's entry into force are critical to the law's success and to the success of future monitoring and enforcement . . . When active enforcement begins, many jurisdictions recommend the use of high-profile prosecutions to enhance deterrence.' These threats are not taken, as one might suspect, from the Martial Law Extraordinary Decree of the German Reich of 1938 or from the arsenal of the unlamented GDR but from a quite innocuous guideline of the Council of the European Union, which can be found in Council Recommendation COM(2009) 328 final, presented by the Commission, and which in the space of 24 pages is at pains, plainly and simply, to establish smoke-free environments. The Commission declares that it is being forced to resort to draconian measures as 'voluntary policies at national level have proved ineffective in reducing exposure to tobacco smoke.'

Its efforts are, of course, intended 'to improve public health and prevent human illness and diseases'. Only someone possessed by the death drive could object to that. There is a commissioner in Brussels who is responsible for such matters but his concerns are much wider. In order to save the morally threatened Europeans from themselves, Commissioner Dalli would like to see cigarettes sold only in discreet packaging and not displayed, as was once the case with condoms and pornographic books. This may be reminiscent of the Age of Absolutism, of the obsessive sexual neuroses of the Catholic Church and of 'under-the-counter' goods in the former

GDR, but one is not surprised. More astonishing, however, is his claim that 650,000 Europeans are killed by smoking every year. That sounds like a statistical miracle; because a few years ago the number is said to have been just as high, although consumption of the weed in question has since declined drastically. (The Commission achieved a similar miracle in its campaign against fine dust, when it asserted that 310,000 citizens fall victim to this pernicious enemy annually.) The Commission has not thought of a general ban on handguns and on motorcycles which, likewise, increase the mortality rate. In this respect, it prefers to follow the example of the United States of America where submachine guns are freely available for sale round every corner but one's not allowed to smoke a cigarette.

III

The Commission's Peculiarities and Those of Its Critics

Our Brussels representatives are unloved. From the Council of Ministers to the Commission, from the European Court of Justice to the lowliest departmental official in salary group AST 1, the esteem in which they are held leaves something to be desired. But why the ingratitude? Where does the aversion come from? Why on earth do most of the inhabitants of this continent do all they can to make life difficult for their custodians? There are probably several hundred million such spoilsports. In Brussels, they're puzzled and can't come up with an answer.

It's noticeable that the objections of the troublemakers tend to concentrate on the trivial. They are directed at the symptoms of their discontent rather than its causes. These include the outrage, stirred up by the media, at the supposedly excessive cost of the Union's officials. The privileges and concessions they enjoy are carefully listed. The Directors General of the highest salary bracket are, it is said, paid almost twice as much as comparable civil servants in Germany. Ten per cent of their earnings are tax-free, as are travel expenses where appropriate and household, child and education allowances. Anyone not working in his or her home country receives a foreign allowance of 16 per cent. The pensions provisions are also generous. The European civil servant normally retires at 63 at latest, but he can also already take early retirement at 55. A Commission insider is reported as saying that the beneficiaries were doing so nicely that 'one would have to force them at gunpoint to move away from Brussels'.

These are strong words, probably too strong. They find ready listeners among all who have a fundamental suspicion of those in power, a resentment which is not of recent origin. It comes of centuries of experience and is always easy to instrumentalize. Such criticism does not only affect cross-border institutions. The same envious cries of protest ring out in any country as soon as the allowances of MPs or the salaries of senior civil servants are due to be raised. No demagogue, as long he himself is not affected, will waste a moment's thought on the fact that the employees of every administration, from department head to head of government, are paid a fraction of what an investment banker or the director of a large company receives, to say nothing of favoured pop singers, professional footballers and TV talk-show hosts, whom no one looks at askance for earning millions.

How expensive are our Brussels, Strasbourg and Luxembourg employees, really? Well, that's hard to say. It's even impossible to say exactly how many there are. In press reports, their number fluctuates between 15,000 and 40,000, probably depending on whether all employees are included or civil servants alone. Perhaps we can rely on the annual report of the European Audit Office? According to its figures, the administrative costs of the EU amount to 6 per cent of the total budget. That would be exactly 8.2 billion euros. On the other hand, people who know something about Austria and not only Brussels say that the administration of the city of Vienna is even more expensive than that of the European Union: it amounts to 11.3 billion euros, about 10 per cent of the municipal budget (2009). That sounds odd until one remembers that a big city has to take care of a great deal that the EU leaves to others, such as refuse collection, social services and many other demands. It's evidently thanks to the snares of statistics or, far worse, in the nature of the thing itself that all calculations of administrative costs remain a closed book to the taxpayer. That, however, is not only true of the city of Vienna but also of the agencies of the European Union.

Under these conditions, one might want to defend the Brussels bureaucrats rather than reproach them. It is surely no pleasure to spend a 60-hour week in a climate of unpopularity, internal conflicts, blockages and intrigues, to say nothing of the professional loss of reality which inevitably threatens every political class and increases with the geographical distance from the remaining inhabitants of our continent. It is petty and uncalled-for to demand that, on top of everything else, such a wretched existence be poorly paid.

A further accusation frequently made against 'Brussels' weighs much more heavily. That is, the tendency of the Commission to intervene in the everyday life of Europeans. Its mania for regulation, which drives many citizens crazy, is, however, not so hard to explain. As Robert Conquest once remarked, every bureaucratic organization behaves as if it were led by the secret agents of its enemies. This form of self-sabotage is regrettable but not by chance; because every expansion of the institution's area of competence holds the promise of more power, more money and more established posts. No one has so far suggested a better explanation for many decisions of our European administrators.

Since the Treaty of Lisbon, the Union already claims the following responsibilities: everything concerning the common market; key areas of economic, health, industrial, regional, educational, pensions and youth policies. Environment, climate, energy, research, technology, consumer protection, immigration and asylum, civil law, criminal law, internal security—no field is left untouched.

Moreover, care has also been taken to include an ominous 'flexibilization clause', with which, in case of need, the Union can empower itself to extend its competencies.

The numerous examples speak for themselves. For instance, limits are laid down for 'hand, arm and overall body vibrations' for someone working with a pneumatic drill. But the Commission also passes judgement on rules for dentures. Which cheese is matured in brine has to be noted on the packaging. The case of the cucumber regulation (1677–88) has become famous. It rules that the 'Extra' grade of this vegetable may only be offered for sale if the curve does not exceed 10 millimetres for every 10 centimetres. The producers' associations of some countries with large agricultural sectors not only supported these criteria but also vigorously defended them. Only after 20 years was the Commission willing to abolish it, along with 25 of the 36 rules it had invented for beans, cauliflower and melons. Whether that might also apply to Regulation No. 2396/2001 will have to be investigated by more competent authorities. It lays down that, with Grade I leeks, 'The white to greenish white part of the leeks must represent at least one-third of the total length or half of the sheathed part'; except in the case of early leeks, because then 'the white to greenish white part must represent at least one-quarter of the total length or one-third of the sheathed part'.

That is not the only regulation in danger of being struck off. Other remarkable showpiece specifications like the Banana Regulation and the Marketing Standard for Apples are at risk. As far as the rules on the minimum size of condoms are concerned, whose 'length was to be no less than 100 millimetres and whose width was to deviate no more than two millimetres from the nominal width', the Commission, presumably after a long struggle, has seen sense. A length of 16 centimetres is at any rate not obligatory; it is merely strongly recommended. The battle against unpasteurized cheese and Frankfurt apple wine, foodstuffs which displeased the authorities, must even be considered decisively lost because, in both cases, the stubborn French and the Hessians too were roused to make noisy protests. There are no signs, however, that the Commission has begun to have doubts about its all-embracing jurisdiction. It is very far from drawing radical conclusions from its small defeats. The production of further regulations is flourishing.

A fine example of its zeal is provided by the Commission Regulation (EC) No. 244/2009 implementing Directive 2005/32/EC of the European Parliament and of the Council with regard to 'ecodesign requirements for non-directional household lamps'. In over 14 closely printed pages it stipulates for all Europeans how they must illuminate their private rooms. It's hard to say what prevails here. Is it conscientiousness? Is it bullying? Stupidity? Capriciousness? Or the slightly sadistic delight in ordering and forbidding? No one knows for sure, not even those responsible for it.

'If I could turn back the hands,
If I could turn back the clock on the wall'

That too has been tackled in Brussels. The Directive of the European Parliament and of the Council 2000/84 ensures that, twice every year, a couple of hundred million people have to fiddle with all their watches and clocks, with the result that their biorhythm plays up for a couple of weeks. Numerous studies have shown that the energy-saving effect which is supposed to be produced is not worth mentioning.

Furthermore, these same inhabitants of the continent who are forced to adjust their clocks and night lights in order to obey the decrees from distant Brussels will, from 2013, have to give a 31–42 digit account number if they want to receive a credit transfer not only internationally but also in their own country. Stipulated will be not only the BIC number with 11 digits but another one called IBAN which consists of between 22–34 digits and letters. In Italy, for example, it has 27 figures and in Malta 31, so that 414,000 Maltese have potentially 3,100,000,000,000,000,000,000,000,000, 000 different account numbers available to them, which are to be refined and made more precise thanks to 10,000,000, 000 BIC numbers. This pioneering achievement, against which there have already been protests, bears the Regulation number 924/2009.

It's unclear, on the other hand, at which airports in Europe the nail scissors, belt buckles, bottles of perfume, shoes and corkscrews of passengers have to be classified as potential murder weapons. At any rate, in this respect, as every traveller knows, exact Euro standards are lacking. No doubt we shall not have long to wait for the appropriate implementation rulings.

In all their tireless interventions in our everyday life there is only one field which remains relatively untouched. And that's culture. The Union has never shown much interest in it. It's already bothersome because it's simply difficult to homogenize. It follows that the Commission has entrusted this department to its least competent member. A glance at the budget which the Union makes available for culture is enough to show why. It amounts to 54 million euros, a fraction of one per cent of the total budget; that's about 11 cents annually for every citizen of the Union. As a comparison: the city of Munich alone affords itself an expenditure of 161 million euros on culture. There are said to be people who deplore this philistine miserliness. That is short-sighted. The less the Brussels departments take an interest in culture the better. Because of their indifference, all those to whom this aspect of human existence matters, whether producers or audience, are spared the presumptuous nannying which other areas of activity have to contend with. Directives on how one should paint, dance and write in Europe are the last thing we need.

In every other field, however, the Union proceeds according to a well-established pattern. First of all, in some discussion paper, there are suggestions and proposals which amount to an expansion of its responsibilities. In a complicated process passing through several levels, these ideas grow firmer until in the end a brand new directive, guideline or ordinance is adopted. Care is taken that the proceedings attract as little attention as possible. Only when, usually much too late, the sounds of public objection have become widespread does the apparatus agree on a tactical retreat. Many years, however, can pass before a nonsensical regulation ends up in the waste-paper basket.

The more abstruse these examples, the more the media like them. Anyone who looks more closely will discover, however, that some of these superfluous prescriptions which discredit the workings of the Brussels apparatus can be traced back to the pernicious and hidden pressure of national interests. It is said to have been a Bavarian provincial government that pressed for the standardization of all the tractor seats of the continent. And it's not an isolated case. The regulation on light bulbs was introduced not for environmental reasons but at the request of the electrical lighting industry. The regulation mania thrives, therefore, not only in the European Commission but also in the many villas and big offices of the lobbyists. There are estimated to be 15,000 of them in Brussels and many observers consider that their influence far exceeds that of a Euro-MP.

But enough of this altogether irksome but hardly life-threatening interference and harassment, which mar the image of the European Union! They are nothing more than symptoms of much deeper congenital defects. But before addressing them, it is advisable to take a look at its inner life.

IV

A Look at the Executive Floors

It is frequently regretted that the citizens of the Union show only a modest interest in the institutions which it has to offer; indeed, that they don't even know the leading figures looking after their concerns in Brussels, Strasbourg and Luxembourg. No one seems to know the numerous presidents, vice-presidents, commissioners (or commissars) and committee chairpersons. Some facts deserve to be better known!

First of all, the President of the European Council. It would be awkward if the public were to confuse him with the President of the Council of the European Union. It is, of course, the former and not the latter council that is made up of the heads of state and government of the member states. Whereas its president is elected for two and a half years, the President of the Council of the European Union holds office for only six months. But, take note! There is no way he can attend all the sessions of this body because the Council meets rather frequently and that too in 10 different guises, in particular as: FAC, ECOFIN, JHA, COMP, ENVI, EXC, TTE and CAP. Out of consideration for the German-speaking public, designations such as JI, BeSo-GeKo, WBF and BJKS are also in circulation, while the French prefer JAI, EPSCO, EJC and PAC. Coordination is the responsibility of the GAC, also called CAG, that is, the Council for General Affairs in which the foreign and European ministers of the member states are represented, who, however, also meet in the FAC which is also known as the RAA. The latter has a further member, namely the High Representative of the Union for Common Foreign and Security Policy, who, although president, regrettably has no vote.

The European Commission which consists of 27 commissioners (or commissars)—one from each member country—likewise naturally also has a president, who, among his many other duties, must also appoint seven vice-presidents, one of whom is at the same time Chairman of the FAC. The President has his own General Secretariat to take care of business. Answerable to it are numerous Directorates General, of which only a small selection can be mentioned here: for example, the EAC, the RTD, the ENTR, the TAXUD, the MOVE, the ECFIN, the ECHO, the ENER, the ELARG, the BUDG, the SANCO, the JUST, the DGT, the HOME, the INFSO, the CLIMA, the AGRI and the SCIC. It goes without saying that each Directorate General is further subdivided into directorates and sections; otherwise, the Director General would be a mere Director.

Equal in status to the Directorates General are a further number of offices and services but, above all, the more numerous Community and Executive Agencies scattered over the whole continent, from Alicante to Vilnius and from Heraklion to Helsinki. It is hard to establish their precise number since there are more with every year. While in 1975 there were only two, today there are at least 36; others are still at the planning stage. Such institutions shoot up from the ground naturally, so to speak, like *Brussels sprouts*. These plants obey the principle of self-similarity and bring forth ever-new sprouts.

Each agency is a legal entity in its own right and has the appropriate committees and auxiliary services at its disposal. At the head there is, in each case, a governing board, on which at least 16 members are at work. Very few, however, are satisfied with this minimum line-up. Here the EU-OSHA outdoes all the rest, a body which devotes itself to health and safety in the workplace. It has only 64 employees. But, to make up, has 84 governing board members.

Only an ill-humoured critic, quite lacking in goodwill towards the Commission, will be sufficiently hardened as to slog through the Commission Directory of the

bodies mentioned above. The superficial reader is advised
to be content with the following representative selection,
which only draws on the first letters of the alphabet.

The Directory lists the ACER, the CEDEFOP, the
CDT, the CEPOL, the CFCA, the CPVO, the EACEA,
the EAHC, the EASA, the EAWI, the ECDC, the
ECHA, the EDA, the EEA, the EFR, the EFSA, the
EIGE, the EIT, the EMCDDA, the EMEA, the EMSA
and the ENISA. That should be enough for the moment.

A completely new body is the European Foreign
Service which, depending on the official language used,
is designated by the acronym EEAS, EEA or EAD. It
is to be staffed by officials from the Commission, the
Council Secretariat and diplomats seconded by the national governments. This organization is headed by the
High Representative for Foreign and Security Policy,
who in addition holds the chair of the Council of
Foreign Relations and is not only a member of the Commission but also one of its Vice-Presidents. His (or rather
her) executive staff includes an executive general secretary with two deputies and a head of administration.

This service offers tempting posts, because EU delegations abroad have something of the glamour of a gen-
uine embassy. Their heads are not only allowed to attach
a CD sign to their car but also enjoy the red passport, tax
privileges and the immunity to which a regular diplomat
is entitled. In future, it is intended that the delegations

should be active in more than 130 countries. But that's still a long way off. For the time being, the 3,645 staff members of the service have their hands full with setting up their organization. In the long term, at least, that will ensure that the Union feels itself adequately represented in the outside world.

But who represents the citizens of Europe in the Union? That is the job of the European Parliament, which has already been in existence for almost 60 years. For its work, it too, of course, requires a president. For sure he largely has representative and ceremonial functions. So that he can fulfil them he is supported by a large apparatus. He also has at his disposal his own spacious dining room in the penthouse above the Parliament building in Brussels. (The mural which decorates the room shows 'The Rape of Europa'.) Some of the load is taken off this dignitary by 14 vice-presidents, so that, if need be, one of them is always on the spot to take the chair.

The MPs belong to different party groups. At present, seven of these groups are officially recognized by the European Union. Each club has its own president. The internal consultations of these groups take place in sessions virtually stuffed full of deputy committee chairs.

We had almost forgotten Luxembourg, a fine-looking city in which further institutions and presidents are to be found. The most important of them is the European Court of Justice (ECJ), which officially, however, is only called the Court of Justice and should by no means be confused with the General Court of the European Union (EGC). Admittedly, both are made up of 27 judges, one from each member country; and both consist of eight chambers of between three to five judges; but only the European Court of Justice can boast of eight Advocates General; the Court of the European Union has to get by without these office holders, so that, from case to case, one of the appointed judges has to jump in to fill the gap. The situation of the European Union Civil Service Tribunal (also sitting in Luxembourg) is again different. This is the court of the public servants of the European Union in which no more than seven judges each carry out their duties for six years.

Naturally, neither of the two bodies mentioned can get by without a president, in each case elected for a term of three years. Additionally, the courts have heads of administration, who are called registrars (Kanzler—chancellors—in German) but who are, in terms of protocol, junior to the judges.

Only a complete layperson could think of taking the European Court of Human Rights with its seat in Strasbourg into consideration in this context. It has nothing to do with the European Union, although it displays the same flag and uses the same anthem. It's a completely different story because it comes under the aegis of the Council of Europe in Strasbourg in which not 27 but 47 countries are represented, including Moldova,

Azerbaijan and San Marino. The Council of Europe is distinctive in that, while it has a General Secretary and his Deputy, it does not have a single president to show for itself. Ultimately the Committee of Ministers and the Parliamentary Assembly call the shots there; the latter is also responsible for electing the judges.

There are a total of 47 judges, each serving for nine years, sitting individually, in committees of three, in chambers of seven and in a Grand Chamber of 17. In contrast to the Council of Europe, the European Court of Human Rights does not lack presidents. Besides the chairman, the Court can show off two vice-presidents and three further section presidents, assisted by a registrar and deputy registrar.

Matters are not quite so clear when it comes to EURATOM, also called EAEC; because this is an organization which, on the one hand, is completely autonomous, that is, legally distinct and operates independently of the EU, but on the other has an identical membership and shares all its organs with it, a miracle that would puzzle every anatomist. Where exactly the president's chair stands is hard to say.

Readily identifiable, however, are the persons at the head of the EuRH, with its seat in Luxembourg, which audits the Union's books, likewise the EWSA and the CoR—these latter are committees which advise the Commission. They, too, do not lack presidents and their deputies; whereas the agencies which have to look after data protection and citizens' complaints regrettably have to manage without such dignitaries.

And what about Frankfurt am Main? It, too, has an organ of the Union. The European Central Bank, unlike most other authorities, enjoys formal independence, for which it is envied by many; for, according to Article 130 of the Lisbon Treaty, it is formally not bound by any instructions from the political sphere. Its Executive Board, consisting of a president, a vice-president and four further members, can refer to the article, as can its Council, to which in addition all 17 central bank presidents of the Eurozone belong; even the General Council, which brings together 27 bank presidents, is asked for its advice. These committees, as is only right and proper, meet behind closed doors. Recently, nevertheless, a quite audible grumbling has been heard from the consultations, ever since the ECB began buying up large quantities of risky state loans from financially shaky member states. Pressure from politicians evidently makes itself heard even where it's not supposed to exist.

The survey provided here may be wide-ranging, but whether it is complete is another matter. A final institution which may be mentioned is the EIB, an investment bank in Luxembourg. It, too, is officially regarded as an autonomous organ of the EU, not bound by the instructions of the Commission. That's nice, even if its Board of Governors consists of the finance ministers and the Board of Directors necessarily includes a representative of the Commission. There are, further, a Management Committee, a General Secretariat, six Directorates, an Inspectorate General and—we had almost forgotten him—a President.

V

Esprit de corps

But, as we know, real life doesn't take place on the executive floors. More important than the countless presidents are, ultimately, the ladies and gentlemen in the second rank, the cadres, the sherpas, whose names never crop up in the news. Anyone who would like to get to know them is well advised to leave behind the tourist zone of Brussels Old Town and get on the metro. Michael Stabenow, who knows the district in which the headquarters of the Union are housed, describes the approach to it better than any travel guide:

> The November day promises no more than the blue plastic pail. If on this morning one steps out of the dimly lit catacombs of Brussels' Schuman Station into the open air, then one is at least forewarned. At the exit, water drips ceaselessly from the ceiling into a pail. Avoiding

the well-filled container, one mounts many stairs in the pouring rain. The escalator has not been working for months and now serves as a receptacle for waste paper, cans and cigarette ends. Welcome to the heart of Brussels' EU quarter.

If any proof were needed that Europe is a permanent building site, it would be provided here. If one turns around, then beyond the chronically jammed multi-lane Rue de la Loi, and beyond a mobile crane, one catches sight of the Berlaymont Building, the formerly asbestos contaminated headquarters of the European Union. It was supposed to be renovated for five years, from 1991 to 1996. Then another eight years passed. Today, the 13 storeys of the glass palace accommodate the 27 Commissioners, their staffs and several departments.

Its floor space is given as 241,515 square meters, including the four basement floors for technical infrastructure and the civil servants' parking spaces.

The origin of the name it bears is not immediately evident either to occupants or visitors. There was a Count Charles de Berlaymont in the sixteenth century who tried to mediate between the Spanish crown and the Geuzes who favoured the Netherlands; as a result, he was imprisoned for a while after the victory of the patriotic party. But in truth the name of the building has nothing to do with the liberation struggle against the rule of the Duke of Alba. The plot of land on the Rue de la Loi which today accommodates the Commission was, until 1960, the property of the Dames de Berlaymont, a community of nuns who ran a girls' boarding school there at the edge of the city. Placed under pressure, first by property speculation and then by the Belgian state, the ladies of the order were forced to take flight to the suburb of Waterloo. The site of the once-idyllic convent garden is now occupied by the Europa Quarter, a kind of extra-territorial foreign body in the Belgian capital. The Berlaymont appears shut off from the outside world. Its enclosure cannot be entered without a plastic ID card on one's lapel and without passing through security channels as at an airport.

It's the same at the seat of the Council of Europe, which is called either the Consilium or the Justus Lipsius Building. Here, too, no one knows anything about the name-giver. For sure, there's his statue in the foyer; but in the train of ministers and in the throng of willing hands there will be hardly anyone who has leafed through the writings of this philologist of the age of humanism, not least because they are written in the Latin of the scholarly world.

Stylistically, both buildings show a surprising lack of ambition. The Consilium, only completed in 1995, already looks somewhat down-at-heel, like the art that decorates it. Anyone looking for grandeur and elegance must expect to be disappointed. Even the desks of the most senior ranks appear rather dreary—no comparison with the Elysée Palace! The office of the Mayor of Brussels with its golden Renaissance decoration puts everything the European Union has to offer in the shade.

Much more interesting than their mean display side is, of course, the inner life of these headquarters. The Austrian writer Robert Menasse went to the trouble of studying it. He spent months hanging around in the long corridors of the bureaucracy, in conference halls and offices, to observe the everyday activities. It seems he is planning to write a novel and has chosen, as its principal figure, a civil servant of the Union. That is a heroic project, on which one can only congratulate him; for it means departing from the narcissistic finger exercises with which so many contemporary authors are preoccupied. There are some who will be surprised by the provisional result of his researches. Because 'in the bureaucratic apparatus, he got to know excellently qualified people, men and women thinking in European terms and who, with wondrous efficiency, serve a highly complex machine for the production of rationality'.

That's what they like to hear, of course. And it's true that, in this world, one can encounter many knowledgeable and committed persons. As usual, they are seldom to be found at the highest levels; those are, not infrequently, occupied by politicians who have been shunted off to Brussels from their native countries because, for some reason or another, they have become a burden to their parties; they are then said to 'have fallen upstairs'. Apart from that, it's accepted that the top positions cannot be awarded on the basis of aptitude. Rather, their allocation has to be negotiated according to proportionality, so that none of the 27 member countries is disadvantaged. Qualification is secondary. It follows that there will never be a lack of chronically overtaxed Commissioners.

It's a different matter when it comes to the civil servants of the second rank. A complicated application procedure which chooses the most competent of hundreds of candidates ensures that virtually no one slips through without expert knowledge and professional experience. It's regrettable that most anthropologists prefer Papua-New Guinea to Brussels, for there a particularly curious field could be opened up to research. Even at first sight it's noticeable that anyone who has managed to reach these spheres sees himself as part of an international elite. These officials represent the reason of state of a state that does not exist. Elevated above the parochial horizon of the member countries, they feel called on to recognize a higher overall interest. There is no lack of diligence in their internal world. Many even display a degree of enthusiasm. In the areas of central importance, at least, a 60-hour week is more the rule than the exception. (That is not necessarily true of the numerous executive agencies and subsidiary services of the Union which, in accordance with proportionality, dawdle their time away, scattered from one end of Europe to the other. At the periphery, far from any supervision, efficiency inevitably decreases. Some of these establishments can unhesitatingly be regarded as job-creation schemes.)

What inspires the best cadres of the EU is not their vanity. Unlike a minister, no chief of cabinet is dependent on TV showing his face. Outside the glass walls of the Berlaymont, hardly anyone knows him. What spurs him on is his sense of mission. It must be strong enough to cope with occasional doubts, to which no intelligent person is immune. At any rate, these are not unimaginative bureaucrats. When one meets such people, one may be occasionally reminded of the self-image of graduates of French institutions like the ENA, the École Polytechnique or the Sciences Po. Unlike the students of the latter, part of the *esprit de corps* of the Union's civil servants is not only effortless mastery of the unwritten rules and of the jargon but also a new form of internationalism. Too close a bond to one's country of origin is considered inappropriate. They are multilingual and attach importance to their own staff being recruited from as many member countries as possible.

It is not only the contact to the city in which they are living that is limited to the absolute minimum. Care is also taken to maintain a formal and geographical remoteness from European everyday life. The aloofness is no mistake: it is even desired, because only in this way can the impartiality of actions be convincingly demonstrated.

The unavoidable consequences are obvious. Isolation and self-referentiality increase with distance. That also means that the decisions taken here are increasingly difficult to explain. It is not doing the eager and principled activists of Brussels an injustice to assume that humility is not one of their strong points.

VI

The Half-Forgotten History

How did things get to this point? To answer the question we can spare ourselves the prehistory. It is unnecessary to dwell on Charlemagne, although the Union likes to adorn itself with his name; it has named a 16-storey glass tower on the Rue de la Loi, which houses various Directorates General, after him. Even less do we need to refer to Napoleon Bonaparte and Adolf Hitler, both of whom failed, albeit in very different ways, to force this continent into a straitjacket.

It would also be asking too much to mention the many people who in the past century had something in mind that they called 'the European idea'. One of its spokesmen was Count Coudenhove-Kalergi who, as early as 1923, attracted attention with a manifesto entitled *Pan-Europa*. Countless idealistic movements, unions, action committees and sects emerged from this idea, each of them understanding something different by it. Inevitably, these groups soon became embroiled in all kinds of rivalries and disputes and their influence among active politicians remained limited.

Things only became properly serious after the Second World War. With the beginning of the Cold War, the European cause gathered speed. In 1946, Winston Churchill fired the starting shot with his famous Fulton speech, in which he not only popularized the phrase 'the Iron Curtain' but also called for a new unity in Europe from which no nation should be outcast. That, of course, referred in the first instance to the Germans and was for that reason alone surprising: apart from the Indians there was no people Churchill liked less than the Germans. Hardly a year after the end of the war, his conclusion that the country in the middle of the continent could not be permanently excluded also represented quite a challenge to Germany's neighbours. A few months later, in Zürich, he stated his ideas more precisely: 'We must build a kind of United States of Europe . . . The first practical step will be to form a Council of Europe. In all this urgent work France and Germany must take the lead together . . . Therefore I say to you: "*Let Europe arise*" ' Of course, with his initiative he was thinking less of the well-being of the Germans than of the Soviet threat. For one thing, he saw that the wartime alliance with the Russians could not be saved; for another, he wanted to prevent a second Versailles. Hence, he firmly resisted traditional French prescriptions which came down to territorial demands on the Rhine and the Ruhr. The Americans and British, who saw the Cold War coming, could not agree to such wishes. Others, who remembered German occupiers only too well, disliked the idea that they had to make their peace with them.

Nevertheless, shortly afterwards, Churchill risked taking the next step. He entrusted his son-in-law, Duncan Sandys, with the organization of a notable event, although one almost forgotten today, in the Dutch capital: the Hague Congress of Europe in May 1948. Churchill himself took the chair at this meeting and gave the opening speech. There has hardly ever been such a strange conference before or since, with over 750 participants from 20 countries. No government was officially behind it and it remains unclear who financed the undertaking. Conspiracy theorists suspect that American agencies had a hand in it.

It was a bizarre mixture of dreamers and tough strategists who gathered there in the Knights' Hall of the Dutch Parliament. Alongside leading politicians such as Daladier and Mitterand, Eden and Macmillan there were not only thinkers like Bertrand Russell, Dennis de Rougement and Raymond Aron but also poets and writers, T. S. Eliot, Ungaretti, Madariaga and Silone among them. Not even the theologists were missing. Martin Niemöller was present, in addition to several Anglican bishops. Such a constellation would be quite inconceivable today.

The German participants enjoyed more than the glorious May weather; they were also happy that, for the first time since the war, they were allowed to participate in the negotiations as equals. Of course, Coudenhove-Kalergi and his followers were also there. All kinds of 'Unions', 'Movements' and 'Committees' with grandiose names and little support argued with one another about their ideas. In particular, the factions of the Federalists and the Unionists were at loggerheads for two days. There was little discussion of economic issues. But all could agree on at least one result: the setting up of the Council of Europe, which took place a year later. While the idealists, however, clung to their visions, the pragmatists agreed on the next political moves in pursuit of their interests.

Three inconspicuous gentlemen who had probably never met before sat in the back rows at the Hague: a retired mayor of Cologne, called Konrad Adenauer; Melvin Lasky, an American journalist who lived in Berlin and was rumoured to have links with the CIA; and a Frenchman by the name of Jean Monnet. The last can hardly be left out of this story, because it was he who took the next decisive step towards European integration.

This man is worth a digression. He did not at all correspond to the idea one usually has of a politician. Old photos show an invariably good-humoured gentleman, chubby and with a faultlessly trimmed moustache, such as one might expect to encounter at a Rotary Club. Monnet never stood for political office in an election. Pleasing the crowd, going walkabout was not something he particularly liked nor did he care for the popping flashbulbs of the news photographers. He always preferred to work behind the scenes, shielded from the public gaze. Given the influence he exercised in the most various fields, his attitude is a fairly unique one. Vanity and thirst for fame, essential driving forces of the political class, were evidently not among his passions.

Was Jean Monnet an adventurer? One might think so when one adds up everything he was involved in: he was an entrepreneur, financier, state commissioner and organizer of an armaments cartel that played an important part in the Allied defeat of Germany in the First World War. Already before that, in 1914, he had concluded that 'where there was organization there too was power'. In war, it was essential 'to turn the market economy into a more rational form of organization'.

Gradually, Monnet built up a worldwide network of connections reaching out to London and San Francisco, Warsaw and Shanghai, Geneva and Moscow, Cairo, Stockholm, Washington and Algiers. He was never dependent on the salaries and pensions that state service provides. He had money enough (although, according to him, the international financial dealings to which he owed his independence always bored him).

Even in 1945—the war was not yet over—Monnet imagined 'a system in which the coal and steel reserves of the Ruhr should be placed under a European authority and administered for the benefit of the participating nations including a de-militarized Germany'. The condition was 'that Europe is united, and not only through co-operation, but through a transfer of sovereignty, endorsed by the European nations, to a kind of central union'—a project which at the time still sounded quite improbable.

One year later, de Gaulle set up the Commissariat générale du Plan for France and put Monnet in charge of it. He regarded this task as *une fonction indéfinissable* and did not hesitate to use it as a lever to drive forward his far-reaching plans. (Incidentally, it is to his appointment that we owe the very French description of com-missaire—commissioner or commissar—of which the Union remains so fond.)

All witnesses remark on Monnet's charm and his clear-sightedness, his flexibility and his patience as well as on the persistence with which, under a veil of bon-homie, he pursued his goals. He always operated as a both discreet and influential wire-puller and whisperer in the ears of the powerful of his time. He never joined a political party. Unlike his inheritors in the European Union, he took no pleasure in creating hierarchies of posts. 'If I was in charge of an administrative apparatus,' he said, 'then I deliberately restricted its size.' He pre-ferred to work in the shadows and in small committees.

On 9 May 1950, exactly five years after the unconditional capitulation of Germany, the French foreign minister, Robert Schuman, appeared before the press at the Quai d'Orsay to announce a sensational plan which unjustly bears his name, because its originator was Jean Monnet. 'If they lack ideas,' said the latter in his dry way, 'the men in power accept those of others, on condition that one grants them paternity. Since they bear the risk, they also need the laurels. In my work one has to forget the laurel wreaths.'

Following his prompter, the minister didn't waste words on the 'European idea' and the countless committees and movements promoting it. Instead, he suggested setting up a European authority to manage the European coal and iron markets. Monnet was chosen as the first president of this Coal and Steel Community, and he was dismissive of the annexation plans cherished by some of his fellow countrymen. He thought as a Frenchman, but he was no nationalist. He was a pragmatist. Like Churchill and de Gaulle, he preferred to integrate German industrial potential, in accordance with the motto: If you can't beat them, join them. He accepted the position as the head of the Coal and Steel Union because he had no other choice; because this first nucleus of the European Union was his creation. When he took his leave of the post, he said: 'What is now well on the way for the coal and steel of the six countries of our community, must be pursued to the final goal: The United States of Europe.'

Yet most of the approximately 270 million citizens of the Union born after 1965 have probably never heard of the man. Perhaps the fading of his name has something to do with what has been called the 'méthode Monnet'. What is meant by that is a very specific understanding of politics. He preferred 'elite decisions established by consensus', in which parliaments and citizens had hardly any say. He thought very little of opinion polls and referendums. But that isn't the only reason his proposals were never popular: the European integration he had in mind was technocratic and interventionist.

Monnet attached little importance to the polite fiction of popular sovereignty. Unlike the visionaries who dreamt of it, however, Monnet always knew exactly what he wanted. He deliberately set his mind on a long-term project which, one intermediate step at a time, following its own internal logic, would lead to an ever-more powerful Union. 'I don't need big funds for that. An office, a telephone and a secretary would be enough for me.'

To him, the European Coal and Steel Community was only an initial stage in securing an economic base for his plan. So much more was at stake: that is, to slowly hollow out the core of political sovereignty of nation-states in favour of transnational authorities. He was, of course, much too smart to openly put this goal on the agenda in the 1950s. Not until much later did it gradually become clear where his plan was leading. At the time, there were very few who could imagine what a sweeping success it would enjoy.

Everything that followed was in line with the premises he had formulated. There was, as early as 1948, the OEEC—the Organization for European Economic Cooperation. Its task was to distribute the Marshall Plan funds, to liberalize trade within Europe and to prepare the way for a Payments Union. It almost goes without saying that here, too, Monnet was closely involved.

The repotting of the Coal and Steel Union into ever-larger containers was executed in numerous steps. As usual, the path was paved with abbreviations which only a few Europeans could decipher; it led from the EEC, the EAEC and EFTA by way of the EEA and the EEC to today's EU.

VI

It's the Economy, Stupid!

This slogan, which helped Bill Clinton win the US presidency in the 1992 campaign, could justifiably be emblazoned on the front of the building on the Rue de la Loi in which the President of the Council resides. Because, despite all the metamorphoses, at its core the Union has remained what, until 1993, it described itself as being: an economic community. In the eyes of its champions, it is not politics that is destiny, as Napoleon believed, but economics. It appears as a God-given force which nothing can hold up, least of all the centuries-old traditions, mentalities and constitutions of the countries of Europe. These facts are regarded as mere hindrances which have to be overcome, precisely because the diverse cultures of this continent stubbornly resist being made to conform.

Ever since the days of the Coal and Steel Union, the project of economic integration has always been driven forward without consideration for the economic, territorial, ethnic and religious differences of the member states—a deafness to history which no Karlspreis (that is, the Charlemagne Award) and no Sunday sermon can cover up.

In order to describe the immanent contradictions which this way of proceeding brings in its train, no recourse to the rhetoric of cultural critique is necessary. The tools of systems theory are sufficient. It states that a reduction in complexity, such as is to be achieved by the economic community, inevitably produces new complexities whose costs may turn out to be so high that they can completely transform the system. That is bluntly put, but clear.

So there is a malicious irony in the fact that it is in the very field which the Union has regarded as its own par excellence that the most dangerous cracks have opened up, that is, in the economy. If the founding states still have a comparable economic profile, then soon an increasing number of shaky members joined up and it was obvious that they were not equal to the unbridled competition of the common market. At first, the weak currency countries tried to save themselves by repeated devaluations. But this solution was open to them only as long as there was no common currency.

In order to paper over the inevitable tensions resulting from this structural defect, the Union did not shrink back from breaking its own treaties. If everything had happened properly and in accordance with the rules, then the Union should never have allowed states like Greece, Bulgaria and Romania to join. The government in Athens was particularly diligent in producing unscrupulously falsified statistics; Eurostat, the Statistical Office of the Union, set up in Luxembourg in the days of Monnet's stewardship of the Coal and Steel Union, was taken in by them for years.

This experience does not stop politicians who like to talk about the 'European spirit' from pleading for the accession of ever-more new members. The fact the Union is thereby endeavouring to expand its field of operations as far as the borders of Iraq and Iran does not seem to bother them.

The resolution to introduce a common currency took such efforts into a new dimension. As usual, the decision was prepared behind the scenes. As long ago as 1979, the then European Economic Community created an artificial currency called the ECU (European Currency Unit) which was intended solely as a clearing unit and which was defined by a basket of currencies.

It is probably not chance that the name was reminiscent of a French gold coin in use from the Middle Ages to the Renaissance. The populace at large only caught a glimpse of this newly created currency unit in the shape of special-issue coins. Even when the ECU was transformed into the Euro in 1999, as pure bank money it remained an abstract category at first. Only on 1 January 2002 did inhabitants of the new Eurozone have it in their pockets. But the views of the people on these agreements were heard only exceptionally, as when the Danes and the Swedes were allowed to make their views known in two referendums which both ended with a rejection. In other old democracies, such as Great Britain or Switzerland, there was in any case no likelihood of a majority for joining the zone.

The Pact for Stability and Growth, as it's called, legally binding since 1997, laid down that the public debt of member countries should not exceed 60 per cent of gross domestic product and new public debt no more than 3 per cent per annum. No one has ever paid any attention to these rules. Italy and Belgium were accepted into the Eurozone in 1999 although their public debts in the year reported on, 1997, stood at over 120 per cent of GDP. Greece later joined on the basis of fake figures, which no one checked. It was not only the weaker states but also the heavyweights like France and Germany which reinterpreted the Pact according to circumstances or simply ignored it. Meanwhile, the Commission predicted that, in 2010, of the 16 Eurozone members just one, Luxembourg, would meet the criteria of the Stability Pact. The public debt of 12 members is over 60 per cent, going right up to 140 per cent. The agreements of 1997 have become a joke.

Another rule in the Treaty, specifying procedure, would have even more serious consequences for the Eurozone. Article 125 states: 'A Member State shall not be liable for the commitments . . . of another Member State nor assume such commitments.' The same goes for the Union as a whole.

Of course, here too there is an ambiguous clause which allows the regulation to be annulled. Article 122 leaves an emergency exit open. According to it, the Council at the suggestion of the Commission can grant financial emergency assistance 'Where a Member State is in difficulties . . . caused by natural disasters or exceptional circumstances beyond its control'. The European Council has used this lever to turn the Treaty on its head.

Since then, there has been an avalanche of new abbreviations. In 2010, the Council established the European Stabilization Mechanism, and within the framework of ECOFIN set up not only the EFSM but also the EFSF. That's one of those favoured acronyms which mean nothing to anyone. It stands for European Financial Stability Facility. 'Facility' is a word that comes from the Latin, meaning more or less 'lightness, dexterity, obligingness'. Since that doesn't sound entirely serious, it has been agreed to simply call the whole thing a rescue package. (Or in German, rescue umbrella or canopy, a metaphor coined by the already mentioned M. Monnet as long ago as 1922, except that he, avoiding any hint of pathos, preferred to talk simply of an umbrella.)

Also part of the rescue, or bail-out, package, in addition to the readiness of the member states to grant favours, are guarantees provided by the European Union and funds from the International Monetary Fund.

The cost of this fantastic instrument which is intended to protect the Union against trials and tribulations, which it itself has brought about, can only be given in terms of 12-figure sums. At the moment, it appears to be about 750,000,000,000 euros, but if that's not enough it can be increased as and when required. So the Eurozone has quietly transformed itself into a transfer union in which every member is liable for all the others without limit.

This contradicts both the spirit and the letter of the Maastricht Treaty; consequently, it's also hard to persuade those who are supposed to pay. So two further favours have been invented. For one thing, the European Central Bank was compelled to buy up state loans of the deeply indebted countries, which are worth much less than they cost. These risky junk bonds swell the balance of the issuing bank. When the moment of truth comes, the member countries will have to pump capital into the ECB.

A second proposal goes considerably further. Appealing to 'solidarity', a slogan that has also seen better days, the President of the Euro Group wants to place loans on the market, so-called euro bonds, which are intended to cover 60 per cent of the monetary requirements of the weaker members. As is so often the case, here, too, solidarity is understood as a one-way street. No one wants to be reminded that the term derives from the Latin *solidus*, a word which once meant as much as 'long-lasting, reliable, well-founded'. (It was also the name of a very valuable Roman gold coin which the Emperor Constantine introduced in the fourth century; in France the designation sank very low, becoming the *sou*.)

If Jean Monnet were still alive, he would no doubt look back on the days of the Coal and Steel Union with some wistfulness. Then it crossed no one's mind to distinguish between a 'real' and an unreal (that is, financial) economy. In his day, it was all about iron and coal, products whose use-value no one doubted. The founders of the first European Union concentrated on the problems of heavy industry. They could not yet have a premonition of a spectre which today haunts not only Europe but also the whole planet. It is the globally operating capital market which threatens to kill off their visions. It drives the helpless politicians of the Union before it like a flock of panicky chickens. Further abbreviations have been unable to change that: for example, the CEBS in London, a kind of banking supervisory body which at the beginning of 2011 was replaced by the EBA, to say nothing of the ESMA in Paris and the ESRB and EIOPA in Frankfurt.

As we know, the financial services, as they're called, make their money with 'products' which are considerably more toxic than the emissions which, until a few decades ago, came out of the factory chimneys of the Ruhr, Wallonia and the Saarland. Controlling them is proving to be much more difficult than specifying the ideal shape of cucumbers, tractor seats and toilet bowls.

The Union can no longer master the spirits it has called up. Instruments which were once commonly used in the event of an insolvency, even when there was a risk of a state going bankrupt, as in the debt crises after the Second World War—moratorium, debt conversion, remission of claims—can no longer even be seriously considered. That would 'unsettle' the markets and could harm the German, British, French and Belgian creditor banks. Whoever is considered 'relevant to the system', therefore, has no need to worry.

If one is to believe the politicians, then speculation alone is to blame for the mess. They talk about this unpleasant phenomenon as if it were a ghost, the presence of which is hard to explain and which is even harder to scare away. Yet it is basic to capitalism. The speculators test the market for its weak points; they respond to the increase in state indebtedness which is the result of political decisions; they assess the economic imbalances resulting from the flaws of the economic and currency union; and they analyse the centrifugal forces which that produces. They know that their actions threaten the euro system. But anyone at the top of the finance industry who knows how to make use of this dilemma can count on high, risk-free profits.

In its hour of need the European Council falls back on a catch phrase which national governments also value. 'There is no alternative to the decisions we're taking.' The capital markets don't need to be told twice. They make fun of the politicians, parodying the slogan with an acronym. It's called TINA and stands for *There is no alternative*.

But the notion of a lack of alternatives offends human reason, because it amounts to a ban on thought. It is a statement of capitulation, not an argument. When the generals lay down their arms it is, as always in such situations, not they who have to come up with the astronomically high tributes demanded by the victors, but the rank and file. To quote Gottfried Benn again: 'Another reshuffle, and one retires to one's estates.' It's always those who are least to blame who end up paying. In what form that happens is secondary: tax rises, pension cuts, inflation, currency devaluation. The prescription is not new: socialization of losses, privatization of profits. It's quite logical that political expropriation follows economic expropriation.

VIII

Entering a Post-Democratic Era

In a notable essay, the writer Robert Menasse, already mentioned above, has attempted to defend the honour of the Brussels institutions. He took several months to penetrate their inner life and came to the conclusion that those working in the cabinets of the commissioners, in the directorates-general, the working groups and committees constituted 'an enlightened civil service apparatus' which 'should justifiably be called a *Josephine bureaucracy*, calmly drawing up . . . decrees and guidelines'.

Other observers prefer other comparisons. Instead of looking back to the age of enlightened despotism, they talk of Jacobin traditions or, even more intemperately, of a *nomenklatura* on the Soviet model.

Menasse does not mince words either when it comes to the political price of the Brussels construction. An

attack on the mechanisms of the Union could hardly be
more radically formulated than his defence. He stresses:

> that the present crisis and the way it is being
> addressed touches on the last taboo of democ-
> racies which believe themselves to be enlight-
> ened. This taboo is democracy itself . . . Can it
> be that democracy as we have laboriously and
> inadequately learned it since 1945, and as we
> have become used to it, simply cannot function
> at the supranational level? That it is the prob-
> lem to which with growing helplessness we ex-
> pect it to find the solution? . . . It is a fact that
> all the states which have joined together in the
> EU are democratic, but it's also a fact that in
> doing so they have at the supranational level
> lost democratic standards which had been
> achieved in the nation states, if indeed they
> have not deliberately surrendered them . . . The
> Lisbon Treaty has brought a few improvements
> compared to Maastricht, but the retrograde
> steps and deficits in democratic politics have
> not been removed, far from it, in fact some
> have been virtually carved in stone.
>
> An example: we can only talk of developed
> democracy when there is a separation of pow-
> ers . . . In the EU, however, the division of pow-
> ers has been done away with. The parliament
> is certainly elected, but has no right to initiate

legislation (or now, after Lisbon, only through the back door): only the Commission has the right to initiate legislation . . . But the Commission is the institution in which, in the end, democratic legitimation is annulled: here an apparatus is at work which is not elected and cannot be voted out and which has abolished the separation of powers . . . In terms of democratic politics, therefore, this triad of Parliament, Council and Commission produces a black hole into which what we used to understand as democracy disappears.

That's Menasse's analysis, to which little needs to be added. The conclusions he draws go far beyond the objections raised in the general discussion of the crisis. 'That is the point,' he writes,

at which perhaps one would have to be prepared to admit, that today it is a mark of progress, a liberation even, if the basic conditions of our life are no longer decided by popular vote . . . And only here, observing the construction and working methods of the EU at close quarters, did the thought occur to me, that classic democracy, a model that was developed in the nineteenth century for the rational organization of nation states, cannot simply be applied to a supranational union, indeed perhaps even impedes it.

That pins down the core problem of the Union. Officially, it bears a euphemistic designation. The 'democratic deficit', as it's called, is considered to be a chronic deficiency disease, apparently difficult to treat, which is both lamented and played down. Yet it is far from being a medical puzzle; rather, it represents a quite deliberate decision of general principle. As if the constitutional struggles of the nineteenth and twentieth centuries had never happened, Council of Ministers and Commission already agreed at the foundation of the European Community that the population at large should have no say in their decisions. By now no one believes any more that this relapse into preconstitutional conditions can be cured by cosmetic corrections. The deficit is, therefore, nothing more than a fancy term for the disenfranchisement of Europe's citizens.

As a result, Europe's actors find themselves in an altogether comfortable position. Unlike the classic state of law, there is, in the regime of the European Union, no proper separation of powers; as Menasse rightly establishes, the Commission has a virtual monopoly of initiating legislation. It negotiates and draws up its guidelines behind closed doors. One may suspect, even if not prove, that the lobbyists active in Brussels have more influence on the decisions of the Commission than all the MPs put together.

The European Parliament can only decide the Budget in agreement with the European Council and a single Council representative can block the Parliament's budget decisions. The classic rule *'No taxation without representation'* is thereby cancelled. The Parliament was directly elected for the first time in 1979. Since then, voter turnout has declined continuously; at the last election, it was 43 per cent. The question why this should be so is raised from time to time. Are the procedural rules to blame, perhaps? The principle of degressive proportionality? The distribution of seats according to the Sainte-Lagüe, the d'Hondt, the Hare-Niemeyer method with the rounded off Hare quota or without it? The use of the Droop Quota, or quite simply the preferential voting system?

It's hard to believe that. More to the point may be the suspicion that hardly anyone knows the diverse party groupings that sit in this Parliament. Quite in the Brussels style they hide behind acronyms such as AECR, ECPM, EDP, EFA, EGP, EL, ELDR, EUD, EVP or SPE which very few voters can decipher.

One doesn't get the impression that the election fatigue of the Union's citizens greatly bothers those in power. They observe, unmoved, the dwindling of the base of their legitimation. The suspicion that it even suits them does not appear too far-fetched; because the passivity of citizens is a godsend for every power-conscious executive. And the national governments don't object much either. At home, they maintain with a shrug that unfortunately they were unable to win the argument against the Brussels decisions. Likewise, the Commission can claim that it is only acting in accordance with the intentions of the member states. In this way, in the end, no one can be held responsible for the consequences.

The results of this procedure have coagulated in the *Acquis communautaire*, a monstrous collection of specifications which no soul has ever read. In 2004, it came to 85,000 pages; today, it will be well over 150,000. In 2005, the *Community acquis* already weighed more than a ton, as much as a young rhinoceros. The French version recently had 62 million words. The *Acquis* is legally binding on all member countries. It is estimated that 80 per cent of all laws are no longer passed by the parliaments of the member states but by the Brussels authorities. No one knows exactly. Strictly speaking, it is not, in fact, as in the classic state of law, a matter of legislation but of directives, guidelines and regulations. That corresponds perfectly to the characteristic authoritarian style preferred by the Brussels authorities.

(Anyone who is not satisfied with these references and would like to be better informed about the legislative side of the European Union should turn to EUR-Lex, a data bank in which all the legal orders of the EU, a collection of around 1,400,000 documents, can be consulted free of charge and without obligation. If the excessive expense of this apparatus of regulation is going to be mentioned, then the salaries and pensions the media get so excited about are the least of it. A little while ago, a then-Commissioner by the name of Verheugen let the cat out of the bag and conceded that the EU regulations for European business cost 600 billion euros per annum. That equals the whole GDP of the Netherlands.)

Nevertheless, the founders of the Union once got so far carried away as to lay down a principle in their treaties which is so sensible that any child can understand it: 'Under the principle of subsidiarity, in areas which do not fall within its exclusive competence, the Union shall act only if and insofar as the objectives of the proposed action cannot be sufficiently achieved by the Member States, either at central level or at regional and local level'. The unfamiliar word 'subsidiarity' describes a basic rule which is hard to surpass in its simplicity: Whatever can be decided in a local authority should remain the business of that local authority; what a region can deal with on its own falls within its area of responsibility; and what the nation state can regulate must be left up to it. 'The EU should only then become active if a problem cannot be properly solved at national level, but only at a European one,' says Roman Herzog, a constitutional lawyer and former German president. 'Really, that should be something taken for granted' and yet 'it's almost entirely absent from the mindset of the Brussels politicians, civil servants and the representatives of associations.'

As so often in politics, this principle has hardly any chance of being realized, and precisely because it is so reasonable. It was never meant seriously anyway. The unfamiliar word has remained unfamiliar in the real world even if it is constantly repeated like a mantra. But since it is in the treaties, it could be that some citizens of the Union ask themselves how things stand with the third element of the classic separation of powers, that is, the judiciary, whose task it is to keep a watch over the implementation of the treaties.

But here, too, Herzog has little comfort to offer. 'There are big problems with European administration of justice. The cause is the European Court of Justice which, on ever-more astonishing grounds, is removing fundamental jurisdictions from member states and intervening in their systems of laws. It has, meanwhile, forfeited a great part of the trust with which it was originally met.' The highest court of the Union, just like the European Parliament, has a fundamental interest in constantly expanding its areas of competence. The fact that this practice also brusquely damages the constitutions of the member states leaves the European Court of Justice cold. It evidently believes it can annul the unchangeable core of the German Basic Law (or Constitution). The German Constitutional Court recently put a stop to that. Since then, the Brussels *nomenklatura* regard the judges in Karlsruhe as annoying troublemakers.

It is not only internally that the European institutions show themselves to be suffering from a megalomania that knows no bounds. Their unbridled expansionist drive is notorious. Countries which make a mockery of all accession criteria were incorporated without a fuss and in defiance of the rules. Our little geo-politicians continue to strive to expand their Europe ever further. Why not push forward as far as the Caucasus and into the Maghreb? It would be so nice to be a world power! Even if the Europeans show little enthusiasm for such plans, that's not something that can be taken into account.

In Brussels, their resistance can only be explained by painting them as an ignorant, but rebellious populace that does not know what is in its own interests. So it's best to not even ask what they think in the first place. The mere thought of a referendum immediately puts the Eurocracy in a panic. The results of a total of nine failed plebiscites terrify all those in authority. The Norwegians, the Danes, the Swedes, the Dutch, the Irish and the French have again and again said no. That will never happen again, if the managers of the Union can help it. It's also bothersome, that the nations that invented European democracy, like the British and the Swiss, find it hard to leave behind this form of government.

Consequently, the spokesmen in Brussels, Strasbourg and Luxembourg have come up with a strategy which is supposed to immunize them against criticism. Anyone who contradicts their plans is accused of being anti-European. This kidnapping of terms is a little reminiscent of the rhetoric of Senator Joe McCarthy and of the Politburo of the Soviet Communist Party: they would slander whatever didn't suit them. One lot talked of *'unAmerican activities'*, the other of 'anti-Soviet' activities. A German politician who tried to get the better of his opponents by saying their behaviour was 'unGerman' would make himself look ridiculous. A prime minister of Luxembourg, however, can evidently permit himself to accuse the Chancellor of a neighbouring country of an 'unEuropean approach' if he doesn't like her decisions; and not so long ago José Manuel Barroso, President of the Commission, claimed that member countries which resisted his plans were 'not acting in a European spirit'. (He wanted to impose a new EU tax and, by way of the negotiations on the Union budget, intervene in the budget rights of the national parliaments through the back door.) It's hard to believe, though, that an unelected governor should be the person to embody the European spirit. It's a fairly abstruse idea that the officials of the Union should decide who is a good European and who is not.

Nevertheless, the European Union can pride itself on a form of rule for which there is no historical precedent. Its originality is that it proceeds without force. It treads softly. Its pose is pitilessly benevolent. It only wants what is best for us. Like a kind guardian, it is concerned about our health, our manners and our morals. On no account does it expect us to know ourselves what is good for us; in its eyes, we are far too helpless and immature. That's why we have to be carefully supervised and re-educated.

We smoke, we eat too much fat and sugar, we put up crucifixes in our schoolrooms, we hoard illegal light bulbs, we hang our washing out to dry in the open where it doesn't belong. Where would it all end, if we could make up our own minds as to whom we wanted to rent our apartment! Is it possible that there are deviationists who pay out company pensions when they feel like it, and that someone in Madrid or Helsinki wants to introduce a speed limit that is not in line with the European norm? Must not exactly the same building materials be used everywhere without respect for climate and experience? Can it be left to each country to decide what happens in its schools and universities? Who else but the Commission should make a decision about what European dentures should look like or European toilet bowls? Would we not have to fear frightful confusion if such questions were decided in Stockholm or London instead of Brussels? What if some local council were to concern itself with the guidelines under which buses and underground trains operate in its town? Such exceptions can under no circumstances be tolerated. The European Union knows everything better than we do.

The Union is certainly the boldest but far from the only attempt to leave such an original European invention as democracy behind; because it is not alone in its tendency to control and to make up our minds for us. It would be unfair to ignore how far other societies have advanced on this path.

In Great Britain, the closed-circuit television surveillance of citizens has reached a degree of perfection of which, in the last century, the KGB and Stasi could only dream. The evangelists of cyberspace have no objections to the communications companies spying out citizens; they quite openly propagate the abolition of the private sphere. They are certain of the applause of all security and police services. *The land of the free*, too, has distinguished itself through some pioneering post-democratic achievements. *Executive privilege* allows the President of the United States to initiate wars, set up concentration camps like Guantanamo, legitimize torture and order kidnappings and targeted killings; in the name of national security, he need fear no parliamentary or judicial investigations. Others again look enviously at the economic success of China, which is supposedly due to the fact that its countless unenfranchised millions have no other choice except to obey the wise decisions of the ruling party.

The enlightened EU is far removed from such models. It does not rule by command but by procedure. Fortunately, it has no army or police force of its own; as far as we know, so far it does not even have a secret service which can in any way match the CIA or FSB. For that reason alone, it cannot be compared to authoritarian regimes such as those in the Arab world, in Cuba, in Myanmar or elsewhere. The Union does not see its task as suppressing its citizens but as homogenizing all living conditions on the continent as discreetly as possible. No new prison house of the peoples is under construction here but a reform school, where a benevolent but strict supervision of its charges is exercised. Ideally, the life of the pupils should be centrally controlled and standardized by a lengthy set of house rules, regulating everything from the amount of housing benefit to a healthy diet. The re-education of 500 million people is a Herculean task, however, and quite a few other regimes have found they bit off more than they could chew in making the attempt. We may doubt whether our guardians are up to it.

The Union really has broken new ground with the form of power it exercises. It is a chimera, in both senses of the word: a utopian project and at the same time a hybrid creature, trying to achieve its benevolent aims, which it pursues with cunning and patience, with absolute authority and pedagogical pressure.

In a classic text of political theory which was published more than 350 years ago, Étienne de la Boétie, a friend of Montaigne, asked himself: How is it possible that men put up with the immaturity imposed on them? 'It is,' he asserts,

> the inhabitants themselves who permit, or, rather, bring about their own subjection, since by ceasing to submit, they would put an end to their servitude. A people enslaves itself, cuts its

own throat, when, having a choice between being vassals and being free men, it deserts its liberties and takes on the yoke, gives consent to its own misery, or, rather, apparently welcomes it. If it cost the people anything to recover its freedom, I should not urge action to this end, although there is nothing a man should hold more dear than the restoration of his own natural right.

La Boétie does not, however, have the non-violent guardianship of an enlightened bureaucracy in mind but the undisguised rule of dictators: 'The more one yields to them and obeys them, by that much do they become mightier and more formidable. But if not one thing is yielded to them, if without any violence they are simply not obeyed, they become naked and undone and as nothing.'

The pathos of this brilliant 18-year-old of the Renaissance is alien to us now, as are the conditions to which the author refers. After all, our guardians are not villains but philanthropists. But it was La Boétie who first recognized that the primary cause of 'voluntary servitude' is habit and that is perhaps even truer under the conditions of post-democratic politics than in the past; because it subjects us to the unbearable lightness of a supervision which penetrates all the fissures of our existence.

In 1975, a clear-sighted philosopher of the twentieth century, Hannah Arendt, already said what needs to be said about that. In a speech given in Copenhagen, she spoke of the

> pressure of the threatening transformation of all government [. . .] into bureaucracies, the rule of neither law nor men but of anonymous offices or computers whose entirely deperson-alised domination may turn out to be a greater threat to freedom and to that minimum of civility, without which no communal life is conceivable, than the most outrageous arbi-trariness of past tyrannies has ever been.

So far, there has been little to suggest that the Euro-peans are inclined to defend themselves against their po-litical expropriation. There is no lack of expression of resentment, of quiet or public sabotage, but on the whole the famous democratic deficit has not yet led to revolt, rather to apathy and cynicism, to contempt for the political class or to collective depression.

So the prospects don't look good, but as the engi-neer in *The Sinking of the Titanic* says:

> Salt water on the tennis court can be quite a
>   nuisance;
> but then again wet feet do not mean the end of
>   the world is at hand.
> People are rather too eager for Doom to come,
>   like suicides looking for an alibi. This is
>   likely to lead
> to a failure of nerve and of reasonable discourse.

Europe has survived other attempts to make the continent uniform. Common to all was hubris and none had lasting success. One cannot make a favourable prediction for the non-violent version of such a project either. All the empires of history flourished for no more than a limited half-life, before they foundered on over-expansion and internal contradictions.

IX

*A Conversation between
A, Monsieur de *** of the Commission,
and B, the Author,
at the Fattoria del Chianti,
Rue Archimède, Brussels*

A: I have heard that you are not very well-disposed to our work.

B: Let me thank you for taking the time to talk to me. I know that you are a very busy man.

A: I am all the more pleased at the diversion which I expect from you. You should try the ossobuco they serve here. It's outstanding. Apart from that, I have been told that you compare the Union to a chimera. I would really like to know what gives you that idea. If I am not mistaken, to the Greeks it was a fire-breathing monster; as punishment for the devastation it caused, lead was poured down its throat. That at least is how it is described in the Iliad. I must admit I find the comparison very exaggerated.

B: You judge like a classicist. I didn't expect that in the corridors of the Berlaymont.

A: When I was young, these things were still taught at school.

B: What I want to get at is that the chimera is a hybrid creature: a lion at the front, a snake at the back and a goat in between. Geneticists and medical men are familiar with the term, too. But that's not really what matters to me. I did some reading of your French classics, because I anticipated that my comparison would not be evident to you. *Brillantes chimères*, writes Corneille; Rousseau speaks of *tendres chimères*. What is meant are all kinds beautiful figures of the imagination. In German or English, the word does not have to refer to a monster either but can mean a dream or a vision. I admit, however, it also describes something that cannot be realized, something adventurous, an illusion or a fancy. That gets a bit closer. And as far as the volcanic aspect of the *chimaira* is concerned, I have never failed to emphasize the non-violent approach of the EU. If there ever was anything fiery here, then it must have been a long time ago. The craters which can be viewed in the neighbourhood are cool and damp. They are nothing more than the sites of new office buildings.

A: A sign that we are only at the beginning. The Union is very young. Seen in terms of history, 60 years are no more than an intermezzo, and what you, often quite rightly, complain about are the aberrations of its adolescence, if not its puberty.

B: Or a sign of hardening arteries.

A: You are doing us an injustice. You are always going on about Brussels. Could it be that you have an emotional aversion to institutions?

B: That's possible. But I haven't much interest in a therapy that would rid me of the feeling.

A: Only—why on earth do you keep on about the European Union? Why do you avoid talking about Rome, Budapest or Dublin? These national governments are not one whit better! Their bureaucracies leave a great deal to be desired. There is no lack of narrow-mindedness and incomprehensible hollow verbiage in one as in the other. I won't even mention the scheming and the corruption I encounter every day. Lobbyists, if you'll allow me to be frank, are like flies, no matter where they turn up, in your country too. Just take a closer look at your tax system, your irrational health and education reforms. Everything of which you accuse us, you find again if you look in the 27 different national mirrors of this European Union.

B: But at least we voted for the people who rule us and as long as we hold on to our constitutions we can also get rid of them again. That is not the case here, where you work.

A: I know what you're getting at. Our eternal democratic deficit. Yes, it's a pity about democracy. But the Austrian you like to quote . . .

B: He's called Menasse.

A: He just has the courage to say the truth out loud. You, on the other hand, avoid admitting it. You prefer to take cover behind all kinds of intellectual authorities from La Boétie to Arendt. Yet Monnet, of whom you have drawn a very sympathetic portrait, already saw the fading of classic democracy coming quite a long time ago.

B: He promoted it.

A: He let out, what everyone suspected, even if, cautious as he was, only to close associates. He didn't make many friends by it.

B: You can't count on me when it comes to the success of your chimera. I'm old enough to have experienced dictatorship myself. And I'm very far from the only one. On the question of democracy, an old saying always comes to mind: 'Wer sich nicht wehrt, lebt verkehrt'—If you don't defend yourself, you're doing something wrong.

A: A fine maxim. But you have to concede that, so far, unrest remains very limited. An amount of grumbling also reaches my office but that won't bring the Union down.

B: 'Let's hope things don't get as bad as they already are,' says Karl Valentin, a Munich wise man from the days of silent cinema and music hall. The Union's facing big problems.

A: I'm the last person to deny it. But is that reason enough to paint a picture of the decline of the West? That should be left to the journalists and the speculators. They like to do it, one lot to push up sales, the others to push their stock exchange profits up higher and higher.

B: Agreed. The apocalypse has always disappointed its prophets.

A: And what follows from everything you claim, whether rightly or wrongly?

B: You're certainly not dependent on my suggestions. You can call on crowds of experts and advisers; I'm neither one nor the other.

A: Why do you think I was looking forward to getting to know you? I'm used to exploiting my visitors by getting their advice. So, please, do me the favour and come out with your observations! What do you propose?

B: You're pushing me into a corner. But I shall respond to your question with a couple of questions of my own. First: Why do the advocates of the Union know only one direction? Straight ahead! Head down and carry on regardless! Is continuing growth a natural law? Is everything that's happened irreversible?

A: Meaning?

B: Clausewitz, the cleverest of all strategists, praises retreat as the most difficult of all operations. Is someone who has got stuck in a dead end and can't turn round not courting his own defeat.

A: So you're thinking of a drastic cure?

B: Let's say, rather: of a diet. Your health commissars reproach the Europeans with getting ever fatter; firm action has to be taken, they say. Perhaps the Union should prescribe something similar for itself? Institutions, too, have a tendency to become overweight. Their girth increases if one doesn't do anything about it. I think a slimming course is called for. As you know, that's a heroic task. No one finds it easy to get rid off superfluous pounds. The administrative apparatus! The civil service employment law! The permanent posts! Expansion as an end in itself is a threat to your own project.

A: What are you driving at? Is the Union supposed to gradually wind itself up?

B: Don't you see how modest my demands of the chimera are, how little I expect of radical solutions? It seems to me I'm almost timid when I come back to the arguments which others already put forward decades ago. 'A multi-speed Europe', 'variable geometry', 'graduated integration', 'Europe à la carte'.

A: You know as well as I do that these weren't just words. Think of the Schengen Agreement and the Currency

Union. These are all agreements that derive from such models.

B: The hardliners only put up with it with gritted teeth. They imagine you can get out of a dead end by banging your head against the wall. But all you get for that is a bloody head.

A: I think you're sounding the alarm far too loudly.

B: If you listen to what people around Europe are saying, you'll realize that it's high time to do something about the impending sclerosis.

A: With all due respect for your pessimism . . .

B: That's not it at all. I'm quite simply paying attention to the real Europe, from which the Union is ever more remote, and there I see no reason to be pessimistic.

A: The real Europe? What do you mean by that? With the best will in the world I don't know what it is.

B: Have we not, even if reluctantly, had to get used to another distinction—that between the real economy and its chimerical counterpart, the economy of the financial markets? It's much the same when it comes to European politics. On the one hand the life of the citizens of the Union, on the other, largely isolated from it, the biotope of the institutions. Is it so hard to distinguish one from the other?

A: Could you be more concrete?

B: Gladly. What I'm now taking out of my pocket is a little black book. A diary, lists of things to be done, a list of addresses. The true state of European integration can be gauged from an inconspicuous object like this which can be found in every home. Many don't need such a little book any more. The telephone has become a know-it-all which replaces it. One person knows, at any rate, how to get hold of the Polish plasterer when cracks appear in the living room wall; another prefers to conceal under the harmless letter A the number of his secret lover, whose name is Alice Zimermans and who lives in Amsterdam; a third knows the porter of a small hotel in Odense. These notebooks are stuffed full of divorced husbands, summer homes, business partners, grandsons, account numbers, teachers and pupils, websites, coin collectors, wine-growers, cleaning ladies, car mechanics, handymen working off the books, dentists, scattered from one end of Europe to the other . . .

A: That's enough! I know very well what you mean. But don't forget that, without the European Union, we would never have got this far.

B: It has accelerated the process and made it easier. That's true. But as far as the integration of Europe is concerned, we, long ago, made ourselves independent of the authorities. Today, civil networks bind us more tightly than all the treaties you negotiate here in Brussels. Millions of threads create interdependencies which elude your control and which you can neither tie nor tear.

A: No one wants to do that.

B: The institutions which want to colonize our everyday lives and make everything in Europe uniform hinder more than help us. They are out to standardize us. Unity is good but diversity is better. Please, leave us in peace with your superfluous directives.

A: You're talking about yourself.

B: I doubt that very much. If I may quote another of my witnesses . . .

A: Go ahead!

B: Odo Marquard, an unusually sensible German philosopher, has said that there are certainly some men who have changed the world but what counts is to spare it.

A: Not exactly an orthodox Marxist viewpoint.

B: If you like. You've been very patient with my diatribes.

A: Patience is something that's needed in my job.

B: Perhaps we can agree on at least one indisputable truth.

A: Let's hear it.

B: Brussels may lie in Europe, but Europe does not lie in Brussels.

A: Whom are you telling? Next week I'm finally making a trip home again, to the little place I grew up in. That's where I find the real Europe you're talking about. The people there are, every one of them, stubborn as mules.

B: And you?

A: I'm just like everyone else. How did you find the ossobuco?

B: Thank you, Monsieur. It was excellent.

ARENDT, Hannah. 2003. *Responsibility and Judgement* (Jerome Kohn ed. and introd.). New York: Schocken Books.

DE LA BOÉTIE, Etienne. 1548. *Discours de la servitude volontaire* (*The Discourse of Voluntary Servitude*). Translated into English by Harry Kurz as *Anti-Dictator*. New York: Columbia University Press, 1942. Available online at www.constitution.org/la_boetie/serv_vol.htm

DEMEY, Thierry. 2007. *Bruxelles, capitale de l'Europe*. Brussels: Badeaux.

ENZENSBERGER, Hans Magnus. 1981. *The Sinking of the Titanic. A Poem*. Manchester: Bloodaxe.

'European Commission' at en.wikipedia.org/wiki/

'European Court of Human Rights' at en.wikipedia. org/wiki/

European Navigator, www.ena.lu

HERZOG, Roman. 2008. 'Stoppt den europäischen Gerichtshof'. *Frankfurter Allgemeine Zeitung*, 8 September.

———. 2010. 'Die EU schadet der Europa-Idee'. *Frankfurter Allgemeine Zeitung*, 15 January.

MENASSE, Robert. 2010. 'Populismus zerstört Europa'. *Die Zeit*, 20 May.

MONNET, Jean. 1978. *Memoirs* (Richard Mayne trans.). New York: Doubleday and Company.

STABENOW, Michael. 2010. 'Das Heer der Lobbyisten'. *Frankfurter Allgemeine Zeitung*, 4 December.

VAUBEL, Roland. 2009. *The European Institutions as an Interest Group*. London: The Institute of Economic Affairs.